SOME COMMENTS ABOUT
SELF-DEFENSE for YOUR  T5-ASR-065

*"...an intelligent, clear-headed approach to self-defense; this is no* macho *manifesto."*

BOOKS WEST magazine

*"...an informative and very readable little book for family use..."*

CHRISTIAN HOME & SCHOOL

*"...a life-boat of competence for a sea of violence...this book should be in every home with young children...and on the Parents' Shelf of every library..."*

CLAIRE FREDERICK, M.D.
Psychiatrist; Consultant
Los Angeles School District

*"...should be widely read by teachers, parents and guidance people...self-motivating...well-organized..."*

ROBERT A. AITCHISON, Ph. D.
Consultant, Neuro-Psychiatric Institute
Reserarch Program (B.A.M. Project)
University of California, Los Angeles

*"...a wholesome, ethical approach for coping with interpersonal conflicts...Highly recommended for children, parents and educators."*

HERMINE KOVACS, M.A.
Marriage, Family and Child Counselor

*"Parents who want their children to avoid the role of bully or victim should have this book."*

FRANCESCA ALEXANDER, Ph. D.
Professor, Social Psychology
California State University, Los Angeles

*"Would that I had attended such a class in my elementary school days!"*

S. STANSFELD SARGENT, Ph. D.
Clinical and Social Psychologist

## BOOKS BY BRUCE TEGNER

BRUCE TEGNER'S COMPLETE BOOK OF SELF-DEFENSE
BRUCE TEGNER'S COMPLETE BOOK OF KARATE
BRUCE TEGNER'S COMPLETE BOOK OF AIKIDO
BRUCE TEGNER'S COMPLETE BOOK OF JUKADO
BRUCE TEGNER'S COMPLETE BOOK OF JUDO
KARATE: Self-Defense & Traditional Sport Forms
KARATE & JUDO EXERCISES
STICK FIGHTING: SPORT FORMS
STICK FIGHTING: SELF-DEFENSE
DEFENSE TACTICS FOR LAW ENFORCEMENT:
    Weaponless Defense & Control
SELF-DEFENSE NERVE CENTERS & PRESSURE POINTS
BRUCE TEGNER METHOD OF SELF-DEFENSE
SELF-DEFENSE FOR BOYS & MEN:
    A Physical Education Course
SELF-DEFENSE FOR YOUR CHILD (with Alice McGrath)
    [For elementary school age boys & girls.]
SELF-DEFENSE & ASSAULT PREVENTION FOR
    GIRLS & WOMEN (with Alice McGrath)
BLACK BELT JUDO, KARATE, JUKADO
AIKIDO and Jiu Jitsu Holds & Locks
JUDO: Sport Techniques for Physical Fitness & Tournament
SAVATE: French Foot & Fist Fighting
KUNG FU & TAI CHI: Chinese Karate & Classical Exercise


Additional titles in preparation

# SELF-DEFENSE FOR YOUR CHILD
Bruce Tegner & Alice McGrath

THOR PUBLISHING CO.   BOX 1782,   VENTURA, CALIFORNIA 93001

**Library of Congress Cataloging in Publication Data**

Tegner, Bruce.
   Self-defense for your child.

   1.  Self-defense.  I.  McGrath, Alice Greenfield,
1917-      joint author.  II.  Title.
GV1111.T422    613.6'6'0240544    76-1856
ISBN 0-87407-514-9
ISBN 0-87407-024-4 (pbk)

<del>&#8592;&#8594;</del>

First Edition: March 1976
Second Printing: February 1977

SELF-DEFENSE for YOUR CHILD
by Bruce Tegner & Alice McGrath

THOR PUBLISHING COMPANY
POST OFFICE BOX 1782
VENTURA, CALIFORNIA 93001

Printed in the
United States
of America

# BRUCE TEGNER BOOKS REVIEWED

BRUCE TEGNER'S COMPLETE BOOK OF SELF-DEFENSE
Recommended for Y.A. in the American Library Association
BOOKLIST

BRUCE TEGNER'S COMPLETE BOOK OF JUDO
"...the definitive text...ideal for instructors and individuals."
SCHOLASTIC COACH

KARATE: Self-Defense & Traditional Forms
"...highly recommended..." LIBRARY JOURNAL
Recommended for Y.A. in the American Library Association
BOOKLIST

BRUCE TEGNER'S COMPLETE BOOK OF KARATE
"Tegner suggest and illustrates changes to bring karate in line
with modern concepts of physical education...invaluable for
teaching karate in schools, colleges and recreation centers."
CAHPER

SELF-DEFENSE FOR YOUR CHILD (with Alice McGrath)
[For elementary school age boys & girls.]
"...informative, readable book for family use..."
CHRISTIAN HOME & SCHOOL

"...intelligent, clear-headed approach..." BOOKS WEST

DEFENSE TACTICS FOR LAW ENFORCEMENT:
Weaponless Defense and Control
"...a comprehensive manual...a practical tool for police academy
programs, pre-service police science programs at the university
level and for the (individual) officer..." THE POLICE CHIEF

BRUCE TEGNER'S COMPLETE BOOK OF JUKADO
"This is the most useful book on the Oriental fighting arts that I
have ever seen" LIBRARY JOURNAL

SELF-DEFENSE FOR GIRLS & WOMEN (with Alice McGrath)
"...The authors' advice is sound and their methods could easily
be practiced..." LIBRARY JOURNAL

SELF-DEFENSE NERVE CENTERS & PRESSURE POINTS
"Students and teachers will find much valuable source material
in this attractive book." SCHOLASTIC COACH

SELF-DEFENSE FOR BOYS & MEN: (A physical education
course) "...recommended for school libraries. The text deserves
inspection by P. E. instructors." LIBRARY JOURNAL

KUNG FU & TAI CHI: Chinese Karate and Classical Exercise
"...recommended for physical fitness collections."
LIBRARY JOURNAL

The authors wish to express
their thanks and gratitude to
the children who demonstrate
the defenses in this book:

FRANCO LARON AMAR
LARRY BURRIS
DAVID CARLSON
JOHN CARLSON
HOLLY HAVERTY
MARLEEN HAVERTY

and to David O. Carlson
for generous assistance

# CONTENTS

# Contents

# Contents

# INTRODUCTION

What pleases us most about the children who have studied with us or who have been taught our method of self-defense is that they have learned appropriate responses to the threat of assault, rather than just learning how to beat up on assailants. They can cope!

These children do not rush into physical defense actions needlessly. They do not submit to aggression passively. They have gained confidence by feeling able to cope, which helps them behave in a way that minimizes the possibility of assault.

When they put physical defense actions into practice, they are successful; they can stop an intended assault and escape from it. They win, but it is more an assertion of control rather than a triumph of force against violence. It is self-control and self-reliance.

Most children learn self-defense fairly easily in a relatively short time. Teaching self-defense to children usually brings quick, satisfying and often dramatic results.

Teaching the physical defenses is not difficult. Most parents have taught their children much more complex and difficult skills many times.

This is not a book about child rearing and we do not intend to categorize child behavior into neat little groups with simple labels. For the limited and special purpose of talking about threat of assault, there are three main kinds of responses: passive, aggressive and assertive.

The passive response is submissive and hopeless. Passive behavior says "I am a victim - do anything you want to me; I won't resist." Passive behavior, though it appears gentle on the surface, can have mental and emotional effects of rageful resentment, fantasies of vengeance, and feelings of powerlessness which sometimes persist into adulthood.

The aggressive response to threat of assault involves exchanging the role of prey for the role of predator; it is counter-violence. Aggressive behavior says: "I have power over you - I have more power than you have."

The assertive response says "I will not be your victim; I don't need power over you. I make my own choices."

In terms of children's relationships: Passive children are pushed around and assent to being pushed around by not taking responsibility for themselves. Aggressive children push others around. Assertive children are neither manipulated nor do they manipulate others.

This book is a guide to help you help your child to be assertive in dealing with physical aggression.

The Problem

We have had many years of experience teaching
children. They have had different backgrounds,
different abilities, different temperaments. We
have taught disabled children, retarded children
and exceptionally bright children.

Explaining why their children were unable to defend
themselves against assault, the parents gave a
variety of reasons - some of which contradicted
the reasons given by other parents. Some parents
thought their children were too small compared
with others of the same age; some parents thought
their children were too large for their age. Some
parents would explain that their children were too
gentle to hurt anyone, even in self-defense; others
would explain that their children were afraid of
retaliation. Frequently, fathers explained that
children had been over-protected by mothers;
just as frequently, mothers complained that the
children had been intimidated by fathers.

Most of the children we taught took class lessons.
This means that in spite of their differences in size,
background, temperament and ability, they were all
taught the same techniques in the same way. Most
of them made excellent progress. And we observed
that, as a rule, a remarkable shift in self-concept
occurred after only a few lessons. This was a
regular occurrence and suggested to us that there
was a common problem, and that this problem had
not been recognized or accurately defined.

What all these children had in common was a feeling
of helplessness. When they began to take self-
defense lessons, the feeling of helplessness was
alleviated.

Self-Defense is Not Instinctive

A number of parents brought children in for self-
defense lessons as a last resort;  a final and
desperate measure.  It was as though the children
suffered from some aberation or deficiency.  The
assumption that any normal child has inherent
self-defense skills is false.  Aggression and self-
defense are learned.  Aggressive individuals get
more than enough instruction through example.

In the interest of health and safety we prepare
children to respond in an appropriate way to a
fire emergency;  we teach them water and traffic
safety.  Although the preventive safety procedures
are fairly simple, we do not make the mistake of
believing that children can automatically or
instinctively cope with fire, water or traffic
dangers.  We know that they must be taught to
behave prudently;  the safety measures must be
explained and rehearsed.

Preparation for dealing with emergencies makes
children less anxious;  they are not indifferent to
the possibility of danger, but they acquire a sense
of competence and are less  likely to panic if they
are confronted with the actual event.

Self-defense can and should be taught with a similar,
anxiety-reducing approach.

JUJITSU SELF-DEFENSE

Although this course is based on ancient forms
of karate/jujitsu, there are  some fundamental
differences between the traditional concepts and
ways of teaching and  our modern adaptation.

In traditional approaches to self-defense, every assault is treated as though it were a serious or deadly attack - as it would be in warfare.

Treating all aggressive actions as though they were vicious assault is inappropriate and counter-productive. Individuals who are taught how to defend against serious assault but who have not learned how to cope with humiliating horseplay, have the choice of overreacting or not reacting at all. Overreacting means using greater force than is necessary. If the child does not react (perhaps through a concern with overreaction), the results can be strong and persistent feelings of powerlessness, frustration, humiliation and rage. The ability to respond appropriately to varying degrees and kinds of aggression is the basis for rational self-defense.

The old way of teaching self-defense involves learning a specific defense for each specific assault. The attack/defense concept makes it necessary to learn hundreds of "tricks," as they are called in jujitsu and kung fu. It is difficult and time-consuming to learn hundreds of attack/defense routines. Having learned them, it is not easy to recall the specific routines; constant, ongoing practice is required.

We have eliminated the concept of hundreds of specific defenses and have evolved a new concept of teaching a "vocabulary" of defense actions. By learning a relatively small group of actions and using them in flexible combinations, it is possible to defend against a great number of common assaults without having to memorize routines. Few of the defenses taught in this course are presented as a sequence of actions done in a prescribed order.

We feel that knowing ten defense actions well is
preferable to learning rigid-sequence defenses.
If your child learns ten defense actions and can
use them without undue hesitation, thousands of
combinations are possible.  By using only four of
the ten actions in any sequence, over five thousand
combinations could be made.  Imagine how long it
would take to learn not five thousand but five hundred
routines, and you will appreciate the advantage of
learning flexible applications of a small group of
defense actions - the "words" with which the
"language" of self-defense is composed.

Additional Reference Material

This book contains all the information you need for
teaching the fundamentals of self-defense to children.
If you want additional, general reference material,
use BRUCE TEGNER'S COMPLETE BOOK OF
SELF-DEFENSE*; if you wish to have additional
reference material on the specific subject of the
effects of hitting at any body target, use SELF-
DEFENSE NERVE CENTERS & PRESSURE
POINTS* by Bruce Tegner.

*Thor Publishing Co., Ventura, Calif. 93001.

DON'T GIVE IN

Among children who have never been taught how to cope with the bully, there is a common worry that if they resist aggression, they will be hurt more than if they submit.

There is incontrovertible evidence that those who passively submit to aggression are hurt more and more often than those who make an orderly resistance.

Resistance does not necessarily mean hitting or physical confrontation. Resistance, if it is immediate and determined, might not have to go beyond the appropriate verbal response or a body movement.

A bully is not ordinarily looking for an adversary. Bullies need victims, safe targets on which to vent rage and frustration.  To make certain that an intended victim is not going to give them any trouble, they test.  The test could be a command or it could be a threatening gesture. At this critical point it is important for the intended victim to <u>refuse</u> to play the part of easy, willing victim.  If the intended victim responds with victim behavior, that tells the assailant that he has selected a safe, helpless target.

Overly complaisant children need special help from you to understand the importance of refusing to be manipulated into the passive victim role.

Further along in the book, there are some suggestions for appropriate responses to the bully's testing threats.

## TELEVISION & SELF-DEFENSE

Children who regularly watch many hours of television have a distorted view of physical violence
and self-defense. They tend to overestimate the
danger of assault in real life and to be confused
about the sources of possible danger of assault.
They tend to identify with extremely aggressive,
punitive behavior, or to identify with extremely
passive behavior. Those who identify with passive
behavior are likely to be the children you are con-
cerned with; they underestimate their ability to cope
with the danger of assault. They tend to confuse the
fabricated world of television with the actual world.

The contents of television programming is not likely
to change immediately, even though there is a
growing realization of its unfavorable consequences.
What you can do is to try to neutralize some of the
effects of television violence on your children.  An
obvious partial measure is to cut down on the number
of hours spent in front of the television. And you can
discuss and explain some of the distortions.

### Reinforcing Helplessness and Despair

In real life, assaults range from somewhat
annoying to moderately serious to extremely
dangerous and vicious.  On television, assaults
are portrayed as extremely dangerous and often
fatal; children are given the impression that
deadly assaults are commonplace.

On the screen, victims rarely demonstrate
effective resistance, giving children the
impression that resistance is either pointless or
impossible, when, in fact, spirited resistance is
successful in many actual instances of attempted
or threatened assault.

On the screen, most women and most children are
portrayed as completely vulnerable to assault.
Against this background of presumed helplessness,
the woman or child who functions competently in a
threatening situation is portrayed as exceptional.
This has the effect of reinforcing feelings of terror
and a sense of powerlessness among children in
general, but among girls in particular.  Boys can.
and some do, identify with the dominant adult male,
but girls are cast in the role of perpetual prey.

Unfortunately, these stereotypes are reinforced in
popular books and in profitable, organized cam-
paigns promoting the concepts of the natural
submissiveness of females and the predatory
nature of males.

## Fight Scenes

Explain to your child that filmed fight scenes are
made to amaze and to thrill - not to instruct.  Fight
scenes are planned, move by move, step by step.
Every part of every fight scene is rehearsed and
the roles of hero and villain are played by actors.
Even when the actors have fighting skills, they
follow the script, which tells them what to do and
when to do it.  Off-stage trampolines are used so
that they can leap higher than any human could in
real life.  Stunt men are paid to fall down as though
they have been struck by forceful blows.  After they
have been hit by the hero, the stuntmen villains get
up and do the scene over again.  They have not been
hurt, they are acting.

How To Use The Book

Before beginning work on the defense actions, read
the entire book.   Become familiar with the material -
the techniques, the concepts, the procedures.   Look
at the photos to get a general idea of what is going
to be covered.

The concepts in this course are just as important
as the physical actions.   Use your discretion about
how and when to introduce and discuss them with
your student.

When you are thoroughly familiar with the contents
of the book, begin practice of the techniques.
Whether you work with the child, or teach children
to work together as partners, pace the practice
sessions to the individual student.   Partners will
take turns simulating the assailant's actions and the
defense actions.   Children of approximately the same
age and same size are ideal partners.   But with
mutual concern and cooperation, differences in age,
size, or sex need not be impediments to good
practice sessions. The teacher sets the mood and
influences the learning environment to a large
degree.

After covering the basic techniques, you need not
necessarily follow the  exact order of the material
thereafter.   It is particularly productive to review
the pictures with your child and select material
which seems especially appropriate for the child's
need.

Hands Off

For the most part, avoid handling your child  in
the practice sessions.   Use verbal instruction as
much as possible; use demonstration instead of
manipulation.

## Length of Sessions

It is more efficient and more satisfying to have
short, frequent practice sessions than it is to
practice for longer periods at greater intervals.

Both student and teacher will accomplish more
in ten or fifteen minute daily sessions than in a
one hour lesson once a week.   School teachers
can handle this problem of scheduling by
organization of the lesson, but parent teachers
are advised to limit the sessions to ten or
fifteen minutes.   Your patience and the child's
concentrated effort and enthusiasm can be
sustained for the shorter period and it will be
easier and more enjoyable for both.

## Encourage

Encourage your child.   Make affirmative comments
and corrections.   Avoid negative criticism.   Use
phrases and a tone of voice which indicate that
you are supportive.   Give honest praise; false
praise undermines confidence and trust.   You can
give genuine praise for effort and for progress.

Children know when they make a mistake.   You
don't have to rub it in by being sharply critical.
"You are losing your balance" is negative and
critical.   "Keep a T-position for better balance"
is positive correction.   "You aren't kicking
properly" is negative criticism.   "Use the edge
of your shoe" is a helpful correction.   Negative
criticism implies dissatisfaction with the child;
positive corrections indicate that you are trying
to help.

Learning vs Pleasing

Some children are so anxious to please their parents
that they cannot concentrate on what they are trying
to learn. They try so hard to win parental approval
that they fail to learn.

You and your child should feel good about the practice
sessions. If, instead, there is irritability or frustration, you may be going too fast, or your child may be
working so hard to please you that there is no energy
left for the lessons. If your child seems more inter-
ested in your approval than in the material you are
trying to teach, try to find a way to reduce the tension.


THE ANXIETY MERRY-GO-ROUND

Children who are desperately fearful about assault
are caught in a double trap. They worry about being
assaulted and they worry because they know their
parents worry about them. Parents who have anxious
children worry because they feel responsible for
their children's anxiety. The children feel guilt
and shame because they believe they are not meeting
their parents' expectations. The parents feel guilt
and shame for not fulfilling their children's needs.
On the merry-go-round of anxiety-guilt-shame-
anxiety, parents and children take a nightmare
ride to nowhere.

As a prerequisite for teaching this course, give
yourself a vacation from anxiety. Focus on reducing
the child's anxiety by explicit, non-ambiguous
acceptance of feelings of fear. The message your
child needs to hear is that you understand those
painful feelings and sympathize with them. Open
acknowledgement and acceptance of a child's fears,
no matter how "unreasonable" they may seem, is
the first step toward reducing anxiety. Hidden fears
persist and grow. Fears which are openly expressed
are more likely to subside.

## SAFETY IN PRACTICE

The techniques in this course have been selected after many years of research, experimentation and teaching. The defenses are effective! They have been proven in use. The purpose of practicing the defenses is to rehearse and learn them; it is not the objective of the instruction to prove the effectiveness of the actions.

There is no need for partners to hurt each other in practice. Working carefully and correctly is more important and more productive than fast or careless work.

The defenses in the text will be described as though they were being applied realistically, but they need not be practiced in this manner. Simulation is appropriate for learning basic technique. It is neither necessary nor prudent to make contact when practicing the hand and foot blows , particularly in the beginning.

The three basic rules of safety in practice are:
   Don't fool around.
   Work slowly.
   Observe the tapping signal.

Tapping Signal

The signal for "stop" or "let go" is tapping with the open hand. The tapping signal should be rehearsed before the defense actions are practiced. One partner grips the other's arm. The gripping arm or hand is tapped twice. The partner who is tapped must release <u>instantly</u>. One partner grips the other around the body, over the arms. The gripped partner taps his own leg. The gripping partner must release immediately.

Tapping is a better signal than a verbal command
to stop the action.  Use of the tapping signal is
positive and it eliminates the need for negative
words and phrases such as "ouch" or "you're
hurting me."  In the practice of choke releases,
if one partner inadvertently hurts the other, the
tapping signal is fast and easy.

Instant release at the tapping signal is fundamental to safe practice: insist upon it!

Work Slowly

Don't rush.  Slow work is a safety measure and it
is a good teaching procedure.  Pace the action to
the ability and needs of the individual students.
Speed of execution  in the practice of a defense
technique is not as important as rehearsing  the
gesture and assimilating the concept.

Working slowly allows greater concentration on
the essential elements:  the students can learn
to perform the defenses with a serious expression,
with controlled body movements and a show of
determination.  If self-defense is to become a
life-long skill, these factors are more important
than  speed of performance.

Serious Business
The best atmosphere in which to teach and
learn self-defense is one in which everyone
is fairly relaxed and friendly; it ought not
to be harsh or authoritarian.  But self-defense
is not a toy and it is not a game.  Don't fool
around with the defense actions.  Fooling
around invites accidents and  it  diminishes
the sense of worth of the instruction.

## SECTION TWO:  BASIC TECHNIQUES

GOOD BALANCE - T-POSITION

Hold your body in such a way that you are not easily
pushed off balance.  If you feel stable, you will
appear confident.

Try this experiment with your partner:

1.  Stand with your feet side-by-side, about eight
inches apart.  Using one finger, your partner can
push at your chest and topple you off balance. With
a vigorous thrust,  you could be pushed onto the
ground.

2.  Now stand in the "T" position:  the forward
foot is placed with the toes pointed toward your
partner:  the toes of the rear foot point to the side.
If you brought your feet together, it would make a
T-shape.  Now bend your knees very slightly and
shift your body weight forward slightly.  In this
position you can withstand a considerably more
forceful push without losing your balance.

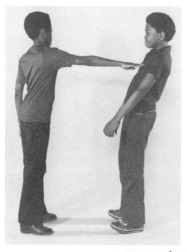

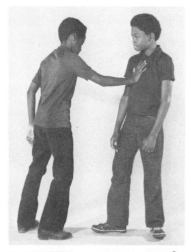

1                                          2

THE CHOP:  An Open-Hand Blow

This is the single most useful self-defense hand blow.
Hitting with the edge of the open hand is easy and
effective.   There are many different ways to use this
basic technique.

In the movies and on television, this blow is called a
"chop." It has been called the judo chop, the karate
chop, the kung fu chop and the jujitsu chop.  No matter
what it is called, it is the same blow.  We call the
open-hand blow a "slash" or "chop" and use these
terms interchangeably.

The advantages of using the chop for self-defense are:
You can use it without necessarily coming within your
assailant's hand reach or punching range.  You do not
have to be a strong person to deliver an effective open-
hand blow.  You can use your right or left hand with
almost equal ease.  You can use the chop with moderate
impact for annoying situations and with considerable
force for serious assault.  You can be ready to use
the open-hand blow without signifying the intention to
fight.

The amount of force you deliver with the chop depends
on how snappy, vigorous and fast you hit.  You do not
have to be "lightening fast" to deliver an effective chop;
with moderate practice you can hit as fast as you can -
which is fast enough for self-defense.

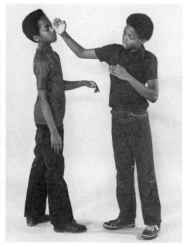

3                                         4

3.  The correct position for the open hand blow called the chop is shown here.  Your fingers and thumb are together -- not spread out.  Your hand is very slightly cupped and held firm, but not rigid.  You hit with the fleshy part of the outside edge of the hand.  Hit with a choppy action, fast and snappy.

4.  When you are first practicing the chop – how and where to hit – merely place your hand at the various body targets so that you will learn the correct position and proper placement.

Holding your hands in the correct position for practicing the chop, touch the various body targets lightly.  Your partner is cooperating with you and simply stands in place to act as a reference.

5                                          6

## WRIST

5.  Your partner extends an arm.  Chop at the wrist.
This action would deflect a reaching or punching arm,
and you could stay out of range of the assailant's hands.
If you chop cross-body, as shown, your action would
deflect the reaching arm outward.  Then, using your
left hand, chop at the same wrist from the outside.
Your partner will then extend the left hand and you
chop at the left wrist, first with one hand and then
the other.

## FOREARM

6.  To find the exact target area on the forearm,
extend your arm in front of you, palm down, and
make a fist.  You will see a mound, just below the
elbow;  squeeze your own arm at the spot, digging
in with your thumb.  It hurts.  Hitting with all your
might at that area causes pain and it deflects the
reaching arm. Chop at the forearm, cross-body,
with your right hand.  Your partner then reaches
with the left hand;  chop at the forearm with your
left hand.

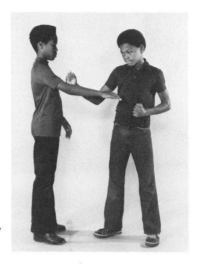

7

ELBOW

7. If you hit into the bend of the elbow, it causes pain and it could bend the reaching arm. Hit cross-body into the right elbow and then practice the same technique using your left hand to chop into the bend of the left elbow.

8

DOUBLE-HANDED SLASH

8. Your partner reaches out with both hands and you chop (slash) with both hands at the same time.

9                                    10

NOSE

9. Hit down onto the nose...

10. ...and up under the nose.

SIDE OF NECK

11. Hit into the side of the neck, a few inches below the earlobe. Slash backhanded, as shown...

12. ...and palm up using the right hand...

13. ...and palm up, using the left hand.

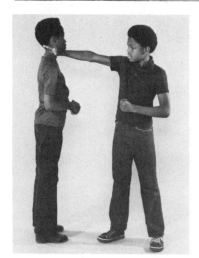

11

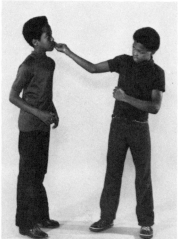

12

13

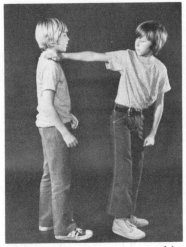 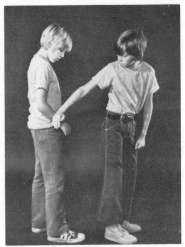

14                                15

SLASHING REAR

14.  You can use the slash to the rear by turning
only the upper part of your body, hitting into the
side of the neck...

15.  ...or at the arm or wrist.

Because the open hand slash (chop) is such an important
basic self-defense technique, be certain that you can do
it correctly.

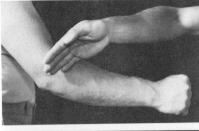

16.  Avoid the mistake
of hitting with your
fingers.

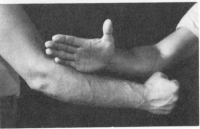

17. Avoid the thumb-
up position.

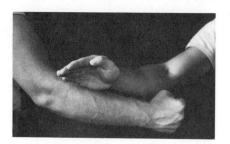

18.  This close-up
shows the correct
hand position.

19

20

HAMMER BLOW

19.  Hitting with the side of your fist down onto the
nose is an easy, effective action.  It is for use when
you are already in close; you should not step in close
to the aggressor if you are out of fist-hitting range.

20.  It can be used even when the aggressor is
considerably taller.

The hammer blow is delivered with a pounding action.

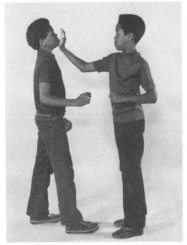 

21                                    22

## HEEL OF PALM

21. If you bend your wrist back and curl your fingers, you are holding your hand in the correct position for hitting with the heel of the palm, the area just above the inside of your wrist. Do not move in close if you can avoid doing so, but if you are already close, a sharp, thrusting heel-of-palm blow up under the chin is an easy and effective action. It is an excellent defense for a small person to use against a larger aggressor.

22. The heel-of-palm blow can also be used up under the nose.

Pushing with the heel of the palm is appropriate for minor annoyances, but against more aggressive assault, the action of the blow should be snappy and energetic.

23                              24

FIST BLOW

23.  The fist blow is an optional technique.  Some people are comfortable using a fist and some are not. Practice it a few times before you decide whether or not it is a suitable technique for you.  The target for the fist blow is the soft mid-body.  If the aggressor is taller and larger, hitting into the face is not practical.  With the palm down, hit straight in.

24.  With the palm up, strike in an upward direction.

 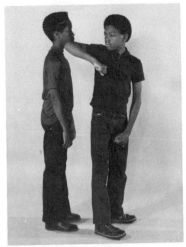

25                                        26

ELBOW BLOW

25.   The elbow blow is most useful for striking toward
the rear.   The two target areas are:  into the mid-
section and...

26.   ...into the head or face.

Though it has limited use, the elbow blow is practical;
hitting with the elbow delivers a forceful blow against
a larger adversary.

BLOCKS & PARRIES

The great majority of aggressive actions, whether they
are annoying, mean or potentially serious assaults,
begin with a reaching-out or punching gesture.  In many
cases, stopping that first action will stop the aggressor.

Remember that the bully is expecting you to behave like
a victim.  If you refuse to submit, by showing that you
can cope with the aggressive action, it changes the
relationship. Since bullies want an easy victory, they
commonly stop aggressing at the first sign of orderly
opposition.

The advantage of stopping the first aggressive action with a block or parry is that you avoid getting hurt or hit and you can do it without making it into a "fight."

There are several good ways to block and parry. Practice all of them and you will then discover the one or two which feel most comfortable for you.

27                                            28

FOREARM BLOCKING

27.  As your partner reaches with the right hand, block cross-body with your right forearm.  This is a procedure which you can practice with moderate contact without danger of injury.  It will help you if you experience the actual feeling of thrusting the arm out of the way.  A vigorous action will deflect the reaching arm.

28.  With your left forearm, using a thrusting action, deflect the reaching arm cross-body.  Avoid pushing; to be effective, the action should be vigorous and lively and followed through.

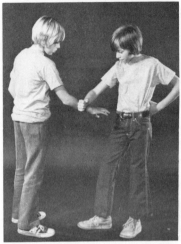

29                                              30

29. With a back-handed action, deflect the reaching right arm with your right forearm.

30. With your right forearm, strike downward on the reaching arm.

Practice all of these blocks using your right forearm and your left forearm; block the reaching right arm and the reaching left arm.

Because the majority of us are right-handed, the possibility of left-handed reaches is less than the possibility of right-handed reaches, but you should practice both. You should be able to block with either your right or your left arm.

31                                                    32

## SLASH/BLOCK

31.  The chop (slash) can be used as a parry or
block.  Slash-block your partner's right arm with
a left-handed outward chop.

32.  Chop-block a left-handed punch with your right
hand, slashing outward.

33                                                    34

33, 34.  Against a right-handed low punch, chop out
with a left-handed slash/block.  Against a low, left-
handed punch, slash out with your right hand.

As a practice procedure, partners take turns
slashing in a rhythmic, one-two-three-four
sequence, the two high and two low punches
shown in photos 31, 32, 33 and 34. At first,
practice slowly; don't try to trick your partner or move faster than the slashing action.
With a little practice, proficiency will develop,
then the procedure can be done a little faster.

After both partners can perform the pre-arranged
1, 2, 3, 4 blocking routine fairly smoothly and with
quick responses, then advance to practice of un-
rehearsed slash/blocking. Partners will then
take turns punching high or low, with the right
or left hand, and the defending partner will try
to respond appropriately. If your partner misses
too many, you are working too fast. Slow down;
increase speed as proficiency increases.

35                                      36

35. Slash-block a right-handed reach with your left
hand, cross-body.

36. Block a right reach, using your right hand for a
back-handed slash.

37                                   38

## SLAPPING PARRY

37.  The slapping parry can be used in much the same
way that the forearm and slashing parries are used -
to stop an intended hostile reaching action or punch.
Avoid trying to <u>push</u> at the reaching arm;  the slap is
snappy and is followed through.  Against a right
reaching arm, slap cross-body with your left hand...

38.  ...and  carry through so that the reaching arm
is well deflected.

Practice slapping a left-handed reach, slapping
cross-body with your right hand.

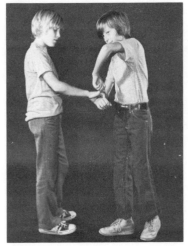 

39                                    40

## FINGER-BENDING RELEASE

39.  The finger-bending release works equally well
against a mildly aggressive action and a serious
assault, such as choking, if you have one free hand.

Your partner grips a wrist.  Grip the little finger
and SLOWLY bend it back.  You must not do this
defense action too fast when you are working with
your partner;  it hurts!  Avoid grasping with your
fingertips;  use your entire hand to grip the little
finger and pull the hand away.

This defense works against a relatively strong grip;
the strength of your hand is greater than the strength
of a little finger,  even when the adversary is bigger
than you are.

40.  Practice the finger release with both hands;
your partner places both hands on your shoulders
or puts both hands lightly around your neck.

41                               42

## THE VALUE OF THE KICK

41.  When two people are approximately the same size, using a fist blow for self-defense puts the defending individual within hitting range of the assailant.

42.  Kicking for self-defense is effective and efficient because:  Kicking is safer;  a kick can be delivered without coming into fist-hitting range.  The leg is stronger than the arm;  even a slight person can deliver a forceful kick with minimum practice. Kicking is a more difficult tactic for the assailant to deal with.

On television, in the movies and in sport karate matches, you may have seen the experts using high kicks, leaping kicks and fancy pivoting kicks. Those kicks are fine for contest and for movie fighting, but they are not practical for you.

The kicks you will use for self-defense are easier to learn and remember and they are safer to use. Your targets for practical defense are:  the shin and the knee.

Before you practice the kicks using your partner as a
point of reference, learn the kicks in solo practice.
Look at photos 44 and 47 very carefully; photo 44
shows the side-snap gesture you will imitate and
photo 47 shows the long-range stamping kick.

SIDE-SNAP KICK

Stand with your feet about shoulder width apart.
Hold your hands lightly fisted and allow your arms
to move as your body moves; avoid a rigid stance.
Raise your kicking foot about 6 or 8 inches and turn
the outside edge of your shoe toward your imaginary
target - the shin of a person somewhat taller than
you. Snap out with the edge of your foot and
immediately place your kicking foot back onto the
floor to avoid losing your balance. Lean your body
back slightly as you kick; avoid leaning forward
toward your imaginary assailant. Snappy action is
the key to the effective use of the edge-of-shoe kick.

43.  The side-snap kick is delivered into the knee or
shin, depending on the space relationship between you
and your assailant.

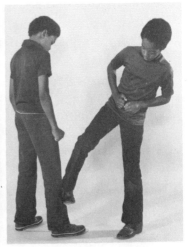

43                                                    44

44. A whipping, snappy kick into the shin is very painful...

45. ...and it can be followed by scraping down on the shin and ending with a stamping kick onto the top of the foot.

46. Practice the side-snap kick very close in to your partner (without making contact, of course) and then as far away from your partner as you can get and still hit with the edge of your shoe. When you are very close in, you will find that it is easier and more comfortable to kick low on the shin; as you move away, you will find that the target area is higher and you might be able to kick at the upper shin or at the knee without losing your balance.

Use the edge of your shoe for delivering the snappy kick to the shin: it is more effective than trying to use the ball of the foot. A toe kick requires greater accuracy than a kick made with the edge of the shoe.

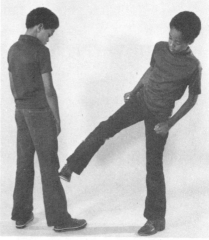

45                                    46

47

## STAMPING KICK

47.  Your imaginary target is the knee of an
assailant somewhat larger than you.  Do not kick
higher than the knee;  the knee is more vulnerable
than the thigh and you can kick at the knee with
greater effect.

Face your imaginary assailant;  turn your non-kicking
foot so that your toes point to the side;  this will give
you stronger balance as you kick.  Raise your kicking
leg, bending your knee and bringing it up toward your
chest;  hesitate for just a second, then stamp out with
the bottom of your shoe directed to the target.  This is
a pounding kick.

Practice to avoid losing your balance as you kick.  Put
your kicking foot down on the ground immediately after
you kick.  Lean your upper body sharply away and that
will increase your kicking efficiency.  Alternate right
and left foot in practice;  you should be able to kick
very well with your strong leg and moderately well
with your other leg.

48. Ordinarily, the kicks
are only used when the
threat is fairly serious.
But if the aggressor holds
your hands, is bigger than
you are and you have no
other way of getting free,
you can use kicks for your
defense.

48

## KICKING TO THE REAR

49. Without turning around, you can kick at an
assailant behind you, using the bottom of your foot.

50. Or, you can kick with the edge of your shoe.
When you practice these kicks, turn your head and
upper body; don't move your non-kicking foot.

49

50

## SECTION THREE

## COMPLETE DEFENSES/ONGOING DEFENSES

Although this method of self-defense is based on ancient forms of jujitsu, there is one major difference between old-style jujitsu and this modern version: Instead of assigning a specific defense for every specific "attack," you are being asked to learn only a very few defense actions which can be used in appropriate combinations to suit many, many different kinds of situations. To learn hundreds of specific "attack-defense tricks" as they are usually called in jujitsu, a long time must be spent learning and practicing the specific "moves." Then, in order to remember them, more time must be spent in practice. When you do not have to remember a specific order of defense actions, it is easier to learn self-defense and easier to remember what you have learned.

ON-GOING SELF-DEFENSE

The response to any assault must be appropriate to the situation. The greater majority of bullying assaults are stopped with the first action. When an assault can be stopped with a single action, such as one hand blow, it is inappropriate to carry on with additional blows.

When an assault or bullying aggression is not stopped with one action, then you should carry on your defense for as long as is necessary. For this reason, you will practice combining the different hand blows in different combinations and you will practice combining hand and foot blows in different combinations.

An on-going defense could consist of a single blow,
repeated as necessary, or it could be a combination of
blows, continued as necessary.  If you repeat one
action with spirit and vigor, that could be effective.
If you can vary the blows and alternate hand and foot
blows, right and left-sided blows, that is even more
effective.

First, practice the combinations that are shown in
the photos:

51.  Using your right hand, deliver a hammer blow
down onto the nose and...

52.  ...follow that with a heel-of-palm blow up under
the chin, using the same hand.

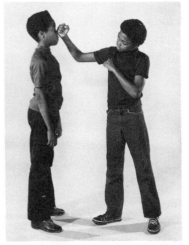 

51                                    52

53                                   54

53.  With your left hand, slash out at your
partner's reaching right hand, and...


54.  ...follow with a right-handed hammer blow
down onto the nose.

55                                   56

55.  Kick low, into the shin...

56.  ...and follow with a heel-of-palm blow up under
the chin.

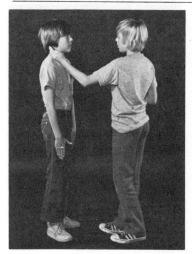

57                                    58

59

57. Start with a left-handed slash into the side of the neck...

58. ...and then deliver a right-handed fist blow, mid-body...

59. ...and finish with a kick into the shin.

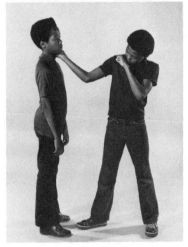

60

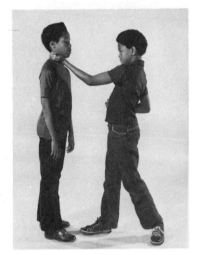

61

62

60.  Hit into the side of the neck with a palm-up slash with your right hand...

61.  ... and follow with a palm-up slash into the neck with your left hand...

62.  ... and kick into the knee as you shift your weight back.

63                                    64

63.  Scrape down along the shin with the edge of your shoe...

64.  ...and deliver an elbow blow into the mid-body as you stamp down on the instep.

Now, go back to the first simple combination shown in photos 51 and 52 and repeat the actions in the opposite order, using first the heel-of-palm blow and then the hammer blow onto the nose.

Repeat the second simple combination in photos 53 and 54, using the right hand to slash at a left-handed reach and follow with a hammer blow with your left hand.

Repeat the third combination in photos 55 and 56, reversing the order;  first hit and then kick.

Repeat the combination in photos 57, 58 and 59, using your right hand to start the sequence.

Practice the combination shown in photos 60, 61 and 62, starting with your left hand.

Practice the combination in photos 63 and 64, first
hitting back with the elbow and then stamping down
on the instep.

Now you are going to be really creative and make up
your own combinations and your own complete, on-
going defenses!  Instead of thinking "What am I supposed
to do now?", you are going to think "What can I do now?"
That saves time. That allows you to respond flexibly
and appropriately.  The bully or assailant is not going
to accommodate you by being aggressive in just the way
you have practiced with your partner.  If you get into
the habit of blocking only right-hand reaches and (just
your luck!) the bully is left-handed, it would slow down
your response.  So, instead of practicing only the same
routine of combinations over and over, you and your
partner will take turns inventing combinations that
are different.

Begin by making up different series of four-count
hand blows.  Alternate right and left hand blows.
Make a series using just your right hand and then
just your left hand.  Using the hammer blow, the
chop, and the heel-of-palm blow, make as many
different combinations as you can by hitting on the
nose, up under the nose, into the sides of the neck,
onto the forearm and wrist, and into the elbow.
You will see that a great number of combinations
can be made using those hand blows.

Then, take turns making up combinations which
include hand and foot blows.

When you have practiced combinations and can perform
them with relative ease and smooth, flowing actions,
then practice for increasing the speed of the actions.
Then practice for the number of actions you can com-
bine into one series.

The foregoing is to give you a sense of confidence in
your ability to cope if the first one or two defense
blows do not stop the assault.   But remember that
MOST assaults can be stopped with the first defense
action!


TRAINING AIDS

Almost all of your practice with your partner will be
simulation - pretending to hit, but not really making
contact.   It is not necessary to hurt each other in
order to learn basic self-defense.   You are not trying
to prove that the defenses are effective, you are
merely rehearsing them for use in an emergency.
You do not have to kick your partner to learn the
correct way to kick.

There are a few practice procedures which can be
used to improve your technical ability, accuracy and
coordination and there are several ways to practice
full-power hand and foot blows without hurting each
other.

Improvised training aids can be made at home and
are very inexpensive.   The training aid for practice
to improve accuracy can be made in several different
ways.   Here are two home-made versions:

Put a tennis ball, or similar-sized rubber ball, in a
sock.   Fasten the ball inside the sock by tying with
a length of clothesline.   For practice of hand blows,
suspend the ball-in-sock so that it is approximately
shoulder high and can swing freely without hitting
anything.   Use a pulley (if there is an appropriate
place to fasten it) or your partner can hold it for
you.

65

Or, you can pierce an ordinary rubber ball with
a screw driver and pass a piece of rope through
the center, making a knot to secure it.  For
practicing hand blows, suspend the ball at your
shoulder height, using a pulley or whatever
ingenious method you can devise for allowing
the ball to swing freely without hitting anything.

Suspend the ball at about your knee height, for
practice of the kicks.

ACCURACY

65.  The ball is a much more difficult target to
hit than any you would be aiming at in street defense.
If you can hit the ball with reasonable accuracy,
you are more than adequately prepared to strike at
body target areas.

66                                    67

Practice hitting the ball gently. If you hit hard, it
will swing wildly and become an impossible target.
Keep your eye on the ball; see how many hits you
can make. This is harder than it sounds or looks.
Practice until you can hit a series of four or more
before you miss. Practice the various hand blows,
the slash, shown...

66. ...the edge-of-fist hammer blow, shown here,
and the heel-of-palm blows as well.

67. Lower the ball to about your knee height.
Practice kicking, using the edge-of-shoe kick and
the bottom-of-shoe kick. Alternate practice kicking
with the right foot and the left foot. Practice to
hit the ball accurately, but gently. Practice to
improve your ability to make contact with the ball
for a series of four kicks or more. Don't be
discouraged if you feel awkward at first; everybody
does.

68                                            69

To practice full contact blocking and hitting, you can
improvise a home-made training aid that is safe and
fun to use.  Start with two pieces of dowel (or similar
smooth, sturdy, 3/4" sticks).

There should be no splinters or edges on the sticks.
Fasten foam-rubber sheeting or toweling around the
sticks so that they are  completely covered.  DO NOT
use pins or metal fasteners.  Sew or tape the padding
in place.  You should be able to hit at the padded area
with full force without hurting yourself.

68.  As your partner extends the stick high, block
upward with a vigorous action.

69.  Your partner extends the stick with his right
hand;  block outward vigorously.

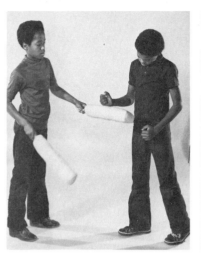 

70                                        71

72

70.  Your partner extends the stick with his left hand;  use a downward block.

71.  Practice back-handed blocks.

72.  Practice cross-body blocking.

FULL-FORCE KICKS

To practice kicking with full force, improvise a
kicking bag which can be hit without hurting
yourself and which will not slide or skid when it
is hit.  A laundry bag or a duffel bag stuffed with
newspapers makes an excellent kicking bag.

Make sure that there are no protrusions, or metal
parts on your kicking bag.  Unless there are thick
seams on your kicking bag, you should be able to
kick it full force, barefoot or wearing shoes, without hurting yourself.  If there are thick seams on
the bag, wear shoes for practice of fully-released
kicks.

Be considerate;  select a location for propping your
bag which allows you practice without annoying
other people. When you are kicking the bag, keep
your kicks at the level of an imaginary assailant's
shin or knees;  with relatively little practice you
will develop all the skill you need for practical
self-defense.


ATTITUDES OF ASSERTIVENESS

Attitude is mental and physical.  Attitude describes
what you think and feel, but it is displayed in the way
you stand, move, and talk, and by your facial
expression.

You can rehearse the outward appearance of assertive
attitudes and you can learn to avoid the outward
appearance of helplessness.

In the following material, the children are acting out the parts of the aggressive person, the assertive person, and the passive person.

With your partner, take turns acting those parts. You will <u>feel</u> the difference when you are using the gestures of assertiveness than when you are using the characteristic gestures of passivity.

73. You can see immediately who is playing the passive role and who is the aggressor in this photo. The passive person, with head lowered and eyes cast down, silently confirms the bully's view of him. He is showing all the outward signs of being a helpless victim.

74. Now take turns responding to the threat of assault by standing in a strong, well-balanced stance: look straight into the eyes of the bully; use a non-threatening but determined-looking hand gesture.

73                                        74

You will discover that the more confident you look
and sound, the more confident you will feel.  If
you have been behaving in a passive manner, it
might take some practice.  Repeat the assertive
response a number of times, until you are
comfortable doing it.

75.  Continue the role-playing, making a verbal
statement that matches your physical gesture.  In
the photo, the hand and body gestures indicate
helplessness.

76.  The body and hand gestures indicate preparation to cope with the threat.

77.  As you take turns acting out the different ways
to respond, exaggerate your gestures.  When you
play the "frightened, helpless victim" role, cower
back; whine; pretend that you are acting on a stage
and that you want to convince an audience that you
are, first, unable to handle the threat of assault...

78.  ...and then, act the assertive role in the
most convincing way.  Remember that you must
use an assertive (not an aggressive) statement to
match the assertive stance.  "Leave me alone" is
an assertive phrase.

75

76

77

78

Make up your own little scenes of passive and
assertive behavior and phrases.  Remember that
being assertive does not mean making counter-
threats, but means giving clear evidence that you
do not intend to accept the role of helpless victim.

79                                          80

GOING INTO ACTION FIRST

Assertive behavior will decrease the possibility of
assault.  We know this from years of experience
with children.  But there are times when the most
assertive behavior is not enough - some kind of
physical response is necessary.  The physical action
need not necessarily be forceful.   Your physical
action should be appropriate to the situation and it
should have the effect of conveying the message:   "I
am not going to allow you to hit me!"

The pictures in this book show the completed assault;
you do not have to wait until you are hit or grabbed or
held.  If you make a strong statement that you do not
want to fight and the other person insists, then you
are not the aggressor, even though you might make
your move first.

79.   Imagine this as a not-too-serious situation.

80.   The bully tests, by making a reaching move.
Don't let that hand touch your body!  Use a slapping
(or slashing) parry to stop the aggressive action...

81

81.  ... and immediately step back and give the
assertive command.

82.  If, in spite of your best effort to avoid physical
confrontation, the aggressor makes a threatening
move...

83.  ... you should be ready to respond with the
appropriate defense action.  You do not have to
wait until you are hit to begin your defense.

82                                    83

84                                                    85

Even when the threat of assault is made from behind
you, you do not have to wait until the assault is
completed to make your defense move.  You can
practice different kinds of responses to different
situations.

84.  Your partner grabs your shoulder;  immediately
turn to see what is happening as you raise your arm
in a defensive blocking action.

Practice this turn-and-guard action when you are
pulled around to the right and when you are pulled
around to the left.  What you are rehearsing is a
guarded stance which protects you, but does not
necessarily commit you to further physical actions.

85.  From the on-guard position, you could use
kicks, or hand blows, if necessary.

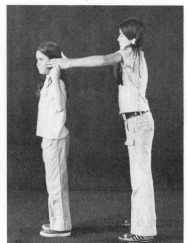

86                                              87

Practice starting your defense when you feel a hand
on your shoulder or arms starting to grab around
your waist.

86.  Before the shoulder grab (or choke) has been
completed, begin the defense.

87.  Practice responding to slight visual cues.
Partners take turns reaching out, first on one
side and then on the other;  the partner in front
reacts by gripping or blocking the reaching hand.

SHOUTING

Shouting is an excellent psychological aid to defense
actions.  Shouting disconcerts and disorients the
assailant.  Shouting gives you the appearance and
feeling of determination and spirit.  Shouting is
unexpected behavior;  victims of assault are expected
to be quiet.  Look directly at your partner;  scream
as loud as you can.  Within reasonable limits,
practice shouting as you perform the defense actions.
Shout anything which feels right for you - a word or
a sound. Shouting as an assertive action is extremely
effective.

## SECTION FOUR

ANNOYING & HUMILIATING ACTIONS

There is no absolutely clear and easy-to-describe
boundary between the teasing of a basically
friendly person and the assault of a mean bully.
Your response to an annoying aggressive action
has to be appropriate to the situation.

When and how do you react? Your honest feelings
are the best guide to the appropriate response.
Most of us can tolerate occasional mildly aggressive
behavior. Friends can engage in rough-and-tumble
horsing around - if there is mutual consent. When
the annoying action causes embarrassment or
shame, then it must be stopped. After you know
how to cope with the aggressive actions, you will
have the confidence to assert yourself.

In most cases, the jolly bully will stop on command.
This has been demonstrated over and over. But if
the aggressive individual does not stop, but
continues to bother you, then use the simple defense
actions.

The examples which follow are only some of the
situations which might fall into the category of
"annoying or humiliating." First practice the
responses as they are shown in the photos. When
you have practiced all the illustrated examples,
think of other possible responses to the same
annoying actions, using the defenses you already
know. Then think of some other examples of
annoying actions and work out the appropriate
responses to them, using the defense actions
you know.

88                                              89

## THE LEANER

88.  Your partner acts the part of the friendly leaner, who won't stop when you make the firm request.

89.  A chop into the side (just below the last rib) is convincing enough to stop the action.

## THE HAND-SQUEEZER

90.  Your partner squeezes your hand and won't let go.

91.  Release the gripping hand by gripping a finger and bending it back.

92.  Or, with an extended knuckle, dig into the back of the gripping hand.

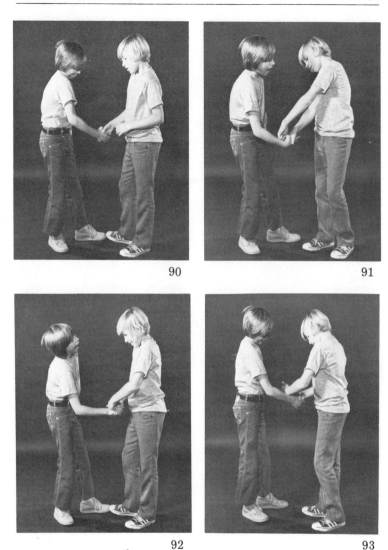

90

91

92

93

93. Or, with the bony edge of your forearm, apply a sawing action against the gripping arm, as shown.

94

95                                              96

## THE PUNCHER

94.   Your partner plays the role of the jolly nuisance
who punches you whenever you meet.   First try the
firm, assertive request to stop doing that.   If that
doesn't work...

95.   ...slash the reaching arm.

96.   Immediately follow that action with the command
"Don't do that.   I don't like it, "   or a similar non-
challenging statement.

## BEAR HUG

97. A double-handed slash
into both sides and a stamp
onto the top of the foot,
simultaneously, or one
action followed by the
other, could be used
in the pictured situation.

97

## WRIST BURN

98. Your partner grips your wrist with both hands
and twists. (Hands twist in opposite directions.)

99. Grip a wrist and twist it to relieve pain...

98                                          99

100                                    101

100.  ...then a slight kick into the shin should effect release.

101.  If necessary, follow with a heel-of-palm blow up under the chin and a stamp onto the instep.

HAIR-PULLING

102.  Your partner grabs a handful of hair and pulls <u>gently</u>.

103.  With both your hands, grip the grabbing wrist and pull toward your head to relieve the pain.

102

103

104

104. Maintain your hand grip as you kick with the
appropriate amount of force. A very slight kick
may convince the bully to let go. If necessary,
kick hard.

If your hair is long and is grabbed at the end,
you can grip your own hair close to your head
and pull toward yourself to relieve the pain; then
kick as appropriate or required.

105

106

107

## TACKLING

105.  To avoid being pushed backwards if you are tackled...

106.  ...drop onto one knee...

107.  ...and hit into the upper back with an elbow blow.

108

109

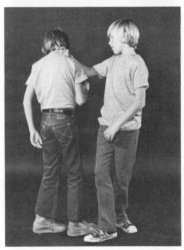

110

KNEE INTO BACK

**108.** Your shoulders are gripped and you are pulled back, off balance; your partner pushes a knee into your back. Trying to struggle forward and out of the grip is too difficult; you would have to be very strong to do that. Without <u>opposing</u> the backward pull...

**109.** ...pivot on the ball of one foot...

**110.** ...so that you are facing the aggressor and can regain your balance. If it is appropriate, one or two hand blows will complete the defense.

SECTION FIVE:  ESCAPES from  GRIPS & HOLDS

## ESCAPES FROM HAND GRIPS

Hand grips, like many other aggressive actions, have
a range of serious intent;  if the person gripping you
does not mean to hurt or harm you, your response
does not have to be as vigorous as if the aggressor
were a mean bully.  The difference in response
is not necessarily in the defense applied, but in
how much defense you use.

## ONE-HAND GRIP

If you are alert and ready to respond, you could pull
your arm free before the aggressor could get a firm
grip.  That would be the easiest way to handle this
situation.  But, of course, you should know how to
break free if your arm has been gripped.

111.  Your wrist is gripped with one hand.  Before
you practice the escape, try breaking free by pulling
away.  Unless you are stronger than your partner,
you cannot get free that way.  Now look at the gripping
hand.  There is an area of weakness in the grip;  where
the thumb and forefinger meet or almost meet (depending
on the size of your partner's hand and the size of your
wrist) the grip is not as strong.  You are going to snap
free in the area of weakness.

112.  Reach over and grip your captured hand...

113.  ...and with a snappy action, pull your arm free
from between the thumb and forefinger, in a sharply
upward and cross-body movement.

111

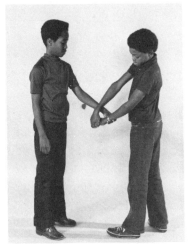

112

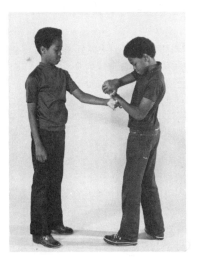

113

114                                      115

116

114, 115, 116.  Practice the same technique when your
partner grips your wrist with the other hand.  Look at
the gripping hand so that you know in which direction to
pull away;  always pull away from between the thumb
and forefinger part of the grip;  use a snappy action to
break free.

 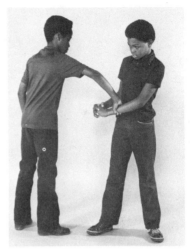

117                              118

Practice the natural-grip releases in slow-motion
first, to make certain that you are doing them correctly.   Even if your partner is stronger than you
are, you will be able to break the grip if you pull
away in the right direction.   It will be very difficult for your partner to maintain the grip with
fingers and thumb.

117.   Your partner grips your wrist or arm with an
un-natural grip.  A natural grip is made with the hand
extended,  thumb up (as though to shake hands);  an
un-natural grip is made with the hand turned over so
that the thumb points down.

Look at the grip.  What has happened to the area of
weakness?  Now it has shifted so that you could not
easily break the grip by pulling  up and away because
you would be  opposing the strong part of the gripping
hand.

118.   Reach under and grip your own hand...

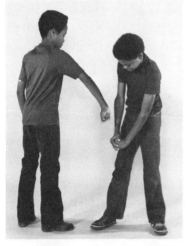

119. ...and break free with a sharp <u>downward</u> snappy action.

119

120

121

## FINGER-BENDING RELEASE

120,121. An alternative defense against a one-handed arm or wrist grip is the finger bending release, which is effective against a considerably stronger individual.

If necessary, a kick into the shin can be used to assist the finger-pulling release.

Practice breaking free from a grip in which the area of weakness is at the side of your wrist. Make your escape from between the thumb and forefinger, no matter where they are positioned on your wrist.

A sharp kick into the shin could assist the release and might be necessary if the grip is too powerful to break with arm action alone.

122                                                             123

## TWO-HANDED GRIP OF ONE WRIST

122. Your wrist, or arm, is gripped with two hands. The arm action is essentially the same as for the two preceding escapes - with one difference: There is no weak line to work against.

123. Reach in between the aggressor's arms and grip your own captured fist.

124

124.  A snappy, vigorous action should effect release.
If it does not, a sharp kick into the shin will hurt and
distract your adversary and allow you to repeat the
arm action for release.


DOUBLE WRIST GRIP

125.  Both wrists are gripped.

126.  Fake a kick into the shin, for distraction, as you
push outward with your arms.  Your captor will oppose
the outward push by pushing inward...assisting you...

127.  ...to go with the inward movement in a snappy,
sharp action;  the direction of your escape is in, up
and out.  Do not try to pull straight back;  make the
escape from between the thumbs and forefingers of
the gripping hand.  If you try to pull straight back,

125

126

127

128

you oppose the strongest part of the grip. When you press out, in and up, you escape at the point of least resistance.

128. If it is appropriate, follow with a hand blow.

129                                    130

DOUBLE WRIST GRIP:  From The Back

129.  Your partner grips your wrists from behind.

130.  Begin with a sharp kick back into the shin, to
distract and hurt your adversary.

131.  Then, with a snappy action, free yourself,
pulling your hands forward and up in a circular
movement.  Avoid making the mistake of trying
to pull your arms forward; unless you are stronger
than your adversary, you cannot free yourself by
pulling with your arms.  By using the snappy, forward
hand action, you work against the weak line of the grip.

132.  Immediately, turn to face your adversary and
indicate your intention to defend yourself from further
aggressive action.

133.  When you can perform the wrist grip releases
moderately well from a stand-still, practice them
with your partner grabbing and dragging you as shown.
Do not try to oppose the dragging action by pulling back;
take a step or two in the direction that you are being
pulled and apply the appropriate release as you walk.

131

132

133

134

134. Practice stepping toward your adversary as you
apply the wrist grip-release against the various kinds
of grips, including the un-natural grip, shown.

135                                   136

BENT-ARM HOLD RELEASE

135.   Your arm is captured and pushed up your back.

136.   First, relieve the pain: Grip your own captured
hand and push down.

137.   Maintain the downward hand pressure as you kick
into the shin...

138.   ...and when you feel the arm hold weakened by
your kicks, thrust your captured arm straight down to
effect release...

139.   ...and turn and hit, if that is appropriate.

137

138

139

The next three situations for which defenses are
shown could range from annoying (the aggressor
is not trying to hurt you, but is teasing or horsing
around) to fairly serious (the person holding you is
trying to immobilize you so that another assailant
can hit you).

140

141

142

BODY GRAB

140.  You are being held
under the arms.

141.  Using kicks into
the shin...

142.  ...and elbow blows
to the face, continue as
necessary to effect release.

Ordinarily, the first blow would result in release,
but be prepared to continue with actions to complete
the defense.

143                              144

OVERARM BODY GRAB

143. You are gripped around the upper body, over the arms. Kick back into the shin, scrape the edge of your shoe along the shinbone and stamp on the instep. This action will hurt and distract the aggressor so that you can follow with the next action. With your hands hooked together (do NOT intertwine your fingers) and your elbows out to the sides (look at the picture to see the arm position)...

144. ...make a sudden, sharp, snappy thrust up, breaking the grip with your upper arms.

If the first thrusting action doesn't break the hold, kick several more times and repeat the arm action for release.

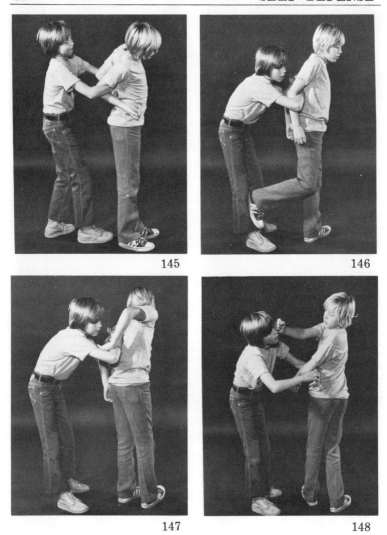

145                                146

147                                148

YOKING

145, 146.  Your arms are pinned as shown.  One kick into the shin would probably effect release.  But if it does not, continue by...

147.  ...twisting your body sharply to one side to free the opposite arm.  The defending partner twists sharply around to the left, decreasing the pressure on the right arm, allowing release.

148.  With a continuous, snappy turning movement, the other arm is freed, and a hammer blow onto the nose completes the defense.

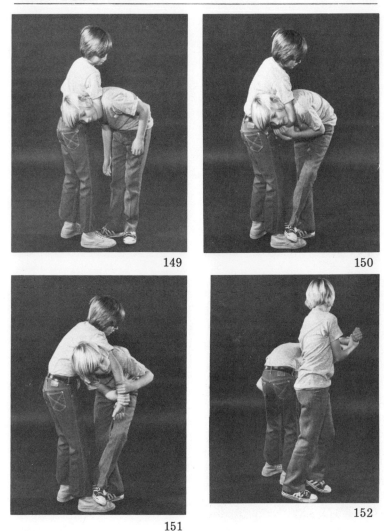

149

150

151

152

HEADLOCK

149.   The defense is the same whether pressure is applied to the head, jaw or neck.

150.   Grip the forearm firmly with both your hands and jerk down as you stamp on the instep...

151.   ...and twist your body sharply, stepping counter-clockwise as you turn.   Maintain your hold on the wrist and...

152.   ...twist it as you turn.

153

154

155

153. If your first snappy pull on the forearm results in complete release, you could...

154. ...step back...

155. ...and place one leg behind your assailant's leg as you thrust up under the chin. Maintain a hold on your partner when you practice this, and be careful! If you trip and thrust vigorously, you could put your partner on the ground!

Practice this defense slowly to learn the correct actions. When you can do this properly in slow motion, speed it up somewhat, but observe the rules of safe practice.

156

157

158

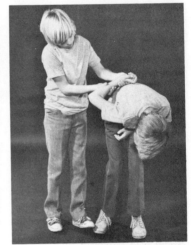
159

SIDE HEADLOCK

156.   The headlock is taken from the side.

157.   The defense is essentially the same as for the preceding headlock. Grip the forearm and pull down sharply as you stamp onto the instep.

158.   Maintain your grip on the forearm as you back out of the hold...

159.   ...and pull the captured arm back and up.

160                                    161

FULL NELSON

160.  Before you begin to practice the escape from the
full nelson, look at photo 160 and figure out what is
wrong with the picture.  Don't turn the page until you
think you know the answer.

161.  Hook your hands together (do not intertwine
your fingers) and press back against your forehead.
This will relieve the pain and allow you to continue
the defense and escape.  Kick back into the shin.

162.  Without attempting to break the hold, take a
deep step to the side, placing one of your feet
outside of the assailant's feet...

163.  ...and then place your knee behind the nearest
knee and buckle with your knee...

164.  ...which should break the hold altogether or
will allow you to use one arm to thrust back against
the upper chest...

165.  ...and complete the escape.

162

163

164

165

The foregoing are examples of some common holds
and captures which you might encounter. After you
have practiced the examples given, think of other
variations of holds and captures which could be
defended against using these techniques.

What is wrong with photo 160?

By now you know that you would not stand there and
allow someone to take this hold. At the first touch,
you would turn and block, or turn and be ready to
kick.

You will learn how to cope with holds and grips so
that you will have confidence in your ability to defend
yourself in the event of surprise action or if you are
not successful in avoiding the hold or grab. But in
real life, many of the aggressive actions you see
pictured in the book could easily be avoided.

Look through the book and decide how many actions
you could avoid by simply stepping away or blocking
the first aggressive move.

KEEP IT SECRET!

Any adversary, even a friendly opponent player in a
game, is a more formidable adversary if you reveal
your plan of action. In a ball game, you do not tell
your opponent where you are going to aim the ball.
For the best preparation in self-defense, do not tell
other people what you are learning and how you
would use it.

Self-defense actions are effective and will work for
you when you need them. Self-defense is not a toy
to show off. If you keep your self-defense knowledge
a secret, you will have the element of surprise in
your favor. Surprise is a big advantage; don't give
it away.

# SECTION SIX:  DEFENSE EXAMPLES

You have already been told that it is not always possible to describe the difference between serious assault and not-so-serious assault just by describing the aggressive action. The intent of the assailant affects the degree of seriousness in some cases, but in some instances, the nature of the assault could result in greater pain or more harm than was intended.

So, in this section there are examples of assaults which are clearly serious and defenses against actions which could hurt you more than your antagonist intends.  Also included in this section are methods of coping with situations which are not really serious in terms of intended harm, but which are more difficult to handle than previously described annoying actions.

Note that the defenses are simple, even when the seriousness of the assault is greater. To complete the defense against a serious assault, you might have to kick harder and repeat the kicks a number of times. You would have to use more vigorous hand blows.  Essentially, the defense actions are those you have already learned to use.

When you have practiced all the defenses which are pictured, think of similar assaults which could be handled in the same ways.

FINGER CHOKE

Choke defenses must always begin with the action
that stops the pain.  In many other situations, it
would not matter in which order you use the
various defense actions, but against a choke,
you should use the pain-relieving action first.

166.  Standing behind you, your partner simulates a
choke.  A firm grip can be applied without digging
fingers into the throat.  Use the tapping signal if the
choke is painful.  You do not have to hurt each other
to learn this defense.

167.  Grip a finger of each choking hand with your
entire hand. Avoid gripping with your fingertips;
grip the entire finger.  Work slowly.  In practice,
grip the little fingers - they are the weakest and
easiest to pull away.  In practice, pull firmly, but
do not use a jerky, snappy action.  Pull until you
have broken the choke. Then, let go of one finger;
maintain your hold of the other finger...

168.  ...and turn and kick, as necessary to complete
the defense.

In actual defense, any fingers you grip can be pulled
back with a snappy, vigorous action to effect release.

166

167

168

FRONT CHOKE

169.  Your partner simulates a choke from the front.
Tap your partner's arm if you are being hurt!  A firm
grip can be taken without digging thumbs into the throat.

170.  Clasp your hands  together as though you are
shaking your own hand;  do not intertwine your fingers.
With your elbows somewhat spread, make a sharp,
thrusting arm action up between your partner's arms...

171.  ...and carry through to break the choke.  This is
not a pushing action;  it is a vigorous, snappy, fast
movement.

172.  Hit and/or kick, as necessary to complete the
defense.

There is another defense (not pictured) you can
practice against the front choke.  When you have
practiced both, you decide which one feels more
comfortable for you.  Your partner simulates the
front choke.  With both hands, slash down onto both
of his forearms or into the bend of the elbows.

169

170

171

172

173                                   174

MUGGING

173. Study the photos carefully, before you practice
the defense. You will see that the escape is almost
the same as the defense against a headlock. The
principal difference is that when you are being choked,
your first action must be to relieve the pain of the
choke. If you stop the choking pain, then you can
carry on your defense; if you try to escape without
stopping the choke, you might increase the force of
the hold. With both hands, grip the choking forearm
and pull down with a sharp, snappy action. This is
not likely to break the choke hold, but will diminish
the pain; turn your head into the bend of the adversary's elbow, to avoid being choked across the
windpipe.

174. Maintaining your grip on the forearm, kick
into the shin, several times.

175. When you feel the hold weaken because of your
kicks, start to <u>back</u> <u>out</u>, still maintaining a firm grip
on the arm...

176. ... and pulling your head back as you take a
step behind yourself...

175                                            176

177                                            178

177. ...to break free and to place yourself behind
the adversary.  You can then push the captured arm
up the back as you pull back on hair...or...

178. ...you can push the arm up the back as you
stamp into the back of the knee for a takedown.

179

180

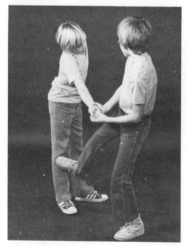

181

179.  Practice another version of the forearm choke release in which you grip the choking arm at the wrist...

180.  ...and with a vigorous downward pull, you break the hold, permitting you to move out...

181.  ...in front of your adversary to kick, as necessary, to complete the defense.

Working slowly with your partner, experiment to
discover why you cannot escape by moving forward
unless the first action pulls the choking arm well
clear of your throat. If you try to escape forward
while the choking arm is in place at the throat,
the forward movement <u>increases</u> the pain of the
choke.

182

SIDE SCISSORS

182. You are held in a side-scissors, as shown.
With the tip of your elbow, dig into the inside of
the thigh.

BACK SCISSORS

183.  You are pinned in a scissors, as shown.

184.  Cross your ankles over the aggressor's legs
and press down with your feet as you raise your
buttocks, bracing yourself on your hands;  the double
action results in painful counterpressure.

In practice, release immediately when your partner
taps.  In defense, stop when the scissors is broken.
Scoot around to face the adversary, as quickly as
possible and rise to your feet facing;  do not turn
your back on the assailant if you can help it.

ON THE GROUND CHOKE

185.  Your partner sits on you and simulates a choke.
Clasp your hands (as though shaking hands with yourself - do not intertwine your fingers) and thrust up
and back with a snappy, vigorous movement to break
the choke.  Hit at the arms and face using appropriate
hand blows until you have completed the defense and
can get up.

This is another example of a situation which might be
altogether harmless horsing around which you could
stop with the first action, or it might be a seriously
threatening assault for which forceful hand blows
would precede the bridging escape, which follows.

183

184

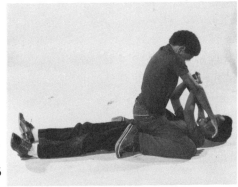

185

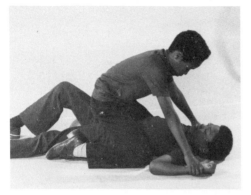

186

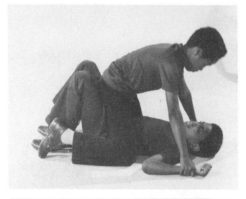

187

188

## GROUND PIN

186. You are pinned, with your arms captured, as shown.

187. Draw your knees toward you...

188. ...and with a sudden, sharp movement, bridge upward...

189

190

191

189.  ...and without hesitation, roll to one side...
toppling your adversary...

190.  ...and continue rolling until...

191.  ...you are completely free.  You could use
hand blows to complete the defense.

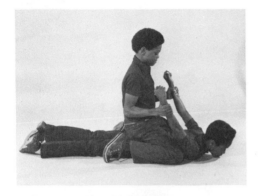

192

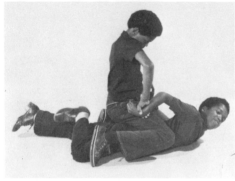

193

PRONE PIN

192.  Your partner sits on your back, holding your
arms as shown.  Unless you are considerably
stronger than the adversary, there is no point in
trying to struggle free.  Relax.

193.  Rock your body to the left side;  the reaction
will be an increase of pressure on your left side
and a decrease in the pressure on your right side.
When you feel the weight shift toward your left
side, draw your right knee up...

194

195

196

194.  ... and with a sharp, sudden movement,
roll over onto your right side...

195.  ... and continue the rolling movement until
you have toppled the adversary off...

196.  ... and rise facing, and ready to use hand
blows if necessary to complete the defense.

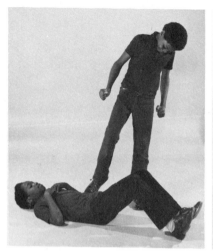 

197                                        198

GROUND KICKING

197.  If you are pushed or fall onto the ground and
an assailant tries to kick you, don't just lie there
passively!  You are in the greatest danger if you
do nothing.  Bullies don't want to be hurt!

198.  Using your hands to brace yourself, swivel
around on your behind;  keep moving so that your
head is always away from the assailant's feet.
Keep going!  Thrashing kicks with both feet can be
delivered from this position and you can prevent
the assailant from hurting you.  One forceful
kick to the knee or shin is usually enough to end
the assault.

When you feel that it is safe to do so, slide back
out of kicking range and rise to your feet, facing
the assailant;  do not turn your back on a kicking
adversary unless you are certain you can run away
to safety.

## LOW KICK

199. The safest and easiest defense against a low kick is a counter-kick, using the edge-of-shoe side-snap or a stamping kick into the shin.

Avoid trying to hand-block a low kick. Attempting to block a low kick with your hands makes you vulnerable because you must come in very close and you must lean over. The counter-kick can be applied without learning over and without coming in too close.

199

200

## KNEE KICK

200. Against a knee kick, hand-parrying _is_ effective. In the attempt to deliver a knee kick, the adversary is already close in. As the kicking attempt is made, use a two-handed slapping, thrusting parry to deflect the kick. You could use a one-handed parry, but a two-handed parry is more efficient. This is not a pushing action; it is a vigorous, slapping thrust.

## HIGH KICK

201.   Parrying a high kick is easier and more
efficient than trying to block or oppose it.  With
a whipping, double-handed parry, you can deflect
the kick and turn the assailant's body around...

202.   ...putting him off balance,  or on the ground,
or turned away from you so that you could follow
with a vigorous kick into the back of the knee.

## BACK-HANDED STICK ASSAULT

203.   Do not try to grapple with or grip a stick, club,
or other rigid extension of the arm;  make your defense
against the arm, not the weapon.

A back-handed swing can be stopped with a double-
handed slash/block;  without hesitation, grip the arm
with both hands and extend your arms stiffly.  You
need only immobilize the arm for a few seconds,
allowing you to...

204.   ...kick into the knee or shin, forcefully, until
the defense is completed.

201

202

203

204

205

206

207

## SWINGING STICK ASSAULT

205.  Block the arm NOT the weapon, with two-handed slash/blocks (or forearm blocks)...

206.  ...and without hesitation, grip the arm and extend your arms fully and stiffly to immobilize the assailant for a few seconds so that you can...

207.  ...kick into the knee or shin, forcefully to complete the defense.  Or you can maintain your hold with one hand and use the other hand to deliver hand blows as you kick.

## TWO ASSAILANTS

208.  You are threatened
by two assailants.

209.  If you can, move
around so that you  are
not  caught between
them.  Out to the side
is the most favorable
position.    Kick into
the knee or the back of
the knee of the person
closest to you and then..

208

210.  ..push that person
into the other one.

209

210

211

212

## BETWEEN TWO ASSAILANTS

211, 212, 213. If you are between two assailants, hit at both of them at the same time using simultaneous hand blows as you kick one and then the other. Keep on hitting and kicking until you have hurt one assailant and push that person into the other one.

213

## MULTIPLE ASSAILANTS - YOKING

214. One person holds you from behind, yoking your arms; a second assailant threatens from the front.

215. Start your defense against the person in front. Kick with vigor until you have hurt that individual and then...          214

215

216. ..effect release using the escape method shown in photos 145-148.

216

## AFTERWORD

A frequently-asked question is: Do children use self-defense after they have learned it? Yes, they do use the instruction, but not in the sense that the question is put, ordinarily. Most of the children who learn self-defense do not have to use the physical techniques; having learned them as back-up actions, they are able to apply the more important part of the instruction: they refuse to play the role of victim and in so doing they enhance their lives.

The feeling of knowing the defenses is as important as the fact. What is enough practice of the physical defenses for one child will not be enough for another. Some children quckly internalize the significance of behavior as the key to assault prevention. These children require a minimum of instruction and practice of the physical defenses to reinforce their assertive responses to the threat of assault.

Children who have become demoralized by the intensity of their despair about the victim role in which they feel trapped, will need more help. Be sensitive to the needs of the individual child and be ready to offer additional help if it is necessary.

REPEAT THE COURSE

After completing the course, if a child expresses or indicates uncertainty about having acquired enough skill, repeat the course. Although the child might, in fact, be quite capable of performing the techniques, there may be a need for reinforcement of feelings. Repeating the familiar defenses will reinforce a feeling of accomplishment.

It is not necessary to learn additional defense techniques.  For most children, it is counter-productive
to introduce unfamiliar defenses if they are not
comfortable with those they have already tried.
Learning a greater number of defenses does not
increase the ability to respond appropriately.  For
practical purposes, it is most efficient to be
thoroughly familiar with a small group of defense
actions.

When repeating the course, do so without suggesting
failure or lack of ability.  Make an honest, positive
statement to the effect that repeating the course will
result in additional assurance and competence.


IMPROVING BODY IMAGE

Body diffidence can be overcome, in many cases,
through a program of acquiring body skills.  Our
experience suggests that the children who benefit
to the greatest degree from practical self-defense
instruction are those least likely to have the
inclination, interest, aptitude or ability to perform
well in competitive sports.  Such children should
be encouraged to engage in solo or non-competitive
physical activity.

While it is true that some children gain confidence
through participation in competitive sport, there
are many who do not.  The traditional wisdom that
team sports build character is being questioned.
There is evidence that the children who enjoy
competitive sports are predisposed to do so;  they
bring qualities to the game rather than take from
it.

According to authorities in the field of sports medicine, there are health hazards in putting children into high risk sports if they are not physically and temperamentally prepared for it. A determination of the child's authentic feelings should precede any decision to train and practice a physical activity or sport. Then, a complete examination by a doctor must be made in order to determine the suitability of the projected project for the individual child. Children have different kinds of bodies and they mature at different rates; what is a health hazard for one child is not risky for another; what is unsuitable for a child at one age might become appropriate at a later time.

For every timid awkward child who emerges from a body-contact or intensively competitive sport experience with increased poise, there are many for whom the experience is a disaster. For every child who wins, there are children who lose; in losing, they feel diminished and demeaned. They are confirmed in their view of themselves as "loser," and this view can, and does, persist into adulthood.

So, in our view, children should not be urged to go into competitive sports. Instead, we suggest gymnastics, swimming, bicycling, jogging, moderate weight training, dancing and so on. In a solo activity, the body-diffident child can improve in health, coordination and agility without being compared with others. A body-diffident child who makes substantial gains in acquiring physical skills might not compare favorably with athletically-inclined children. Making comparisons, which is inevitable in competition, is irrelevant and counter-productive.

Games like tennis, ping-pong and handball can be useful for children if they are paired with opponents of similar ability and if the pressure to win does not interfere with the pleasure of playing.  In order to benefit the body-diffident child, games must be fun, not punishment.

A strong and flexible body is the objective.  To meet this objective, self-discipline and goals set to the individual's needs are reasonable alternatives to team discipline and team play. Self-improvement is a reasonable alternative to winning a game, and requires dedication on the part of the child and encouragement from the parent.

Children who are worried, fearful and filled with anxiety, need relief from their distress.  Physical activity, of the appropriate kind, can give them some relief - mental and physical - and at the same time it can be a vehicle for making progress toward feelings of self-respect and self-control.

Another advantage of solo activites over team sports is that they allow progress to be made at a rate which is appropriate for the individual.

Finally, because solo physical activities (and those in which competition is secondary to the fun of playing) are more likely to become life long pleasures, they offer greater opportunities for the full development of mental and physical health potentials.

# INDEX

**BRUCE TEGNER BOOKS ARE SOLD IN BOOKSTORES THROUGHOUT THE WORLD**

If your book or magazine dealer does not have the other titles you want, he can order them for you, or you can order direct from the publisher.

For description of all the books by Bruce Tegner, and order form, write to:

THOR BOOKS
Box 1782
Ventura, Calif. 93001